Eye Love You

Poems by
Charlie Toth

Eye Love You

Poems by
Charlie Toth

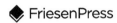 FriesenPress

Suite 300 - 990 Fort St
Victoria, BC, V8V 3K2
Canada

www.friesenpress.com

Copyright © 2019 by Charlie Toth
First Edition — 2019

Mark Klaamas (cover design and photos)
Marsha Robinson (cover and photos including author pic)
Adrienne Dier (poem pictures)
Pierre-Paul Huet (poem pictures)
Jason Matthews (content editing)

www.eyeloveyoupoems.net

All rights reserved.

No part of this publication may be reproduced in any form, or by any means, electronic or mechanical, including photocopying, recording, or any information browsing, storage, or retrieval system, without permission in writing from FriesenPress.

ISBN
978-1-5255-3506-2 (Hardcover)
978-1-5255-3507-9 (Paperback)
978-1-5255-3508-6 (eBook)

1. POETRY

Distributed to the trade by The Ingram Book Company

To:

Andrew Toth
Kyle Toth

You are both Deep,
Funny, Clever, Caring,
Inquisitive, Smart and
Kind. Never lose that!

Eye Love You!

Daddy

Table of Contents

1	AS WE SLEEP	60	LONG TO BELONG
2	BETTER OR BITTER	61	LOVE LOVE!
4	BREAKFAST IN BED	63	LOVE NOTES
6	BRIDGE TO THE WILLOW TREE	64	LOVE OF A LIFETIME
		67	LULLABY FOR WOLVES
8	BROKE AND BROKEN	68	MEAL FOR ONE
10	CHRISTMAS ALONE	69	MISS THE GIFTS
12	CHRISTMAS LOVE	71	MOTHER LIKE NO OTHER
14	DEEP	73	MOTHER'S DAY FUN
16	DON'T ENVY OUR LOVE	74	NO CLUE AT ALL
18	DRAGON	76	PETRICHOR
21	EYE LOVE YOU	78	POPPY IS HERE
23	FATHER OR DAD	79	RUNNING FROM YOURSELF
24	FLOWER THAT I LOVED	82	SEND THE SAND
26	FORK IN THE ROAD	85	SHE WAS SURE
28	FRIENDS FIRST	87	STRENGTH FROM TEARS
30	GONE	89	TAKE HER BACK
32	GOOD MORNING TEXT	90	TEARS OF A CLOWN
34	HAND TO HOLD	91	THE FIVE W'S
36	HER EYES	92	THE OCEAN'S SPECIAL GIFTS
37	HOLD ON TIGHT		
39	HOPE	94	THE RESCUER
42	HUGS AND KISSES	96	THEY ARE NOT COMING
44	I CAN'T LET YOU GO	97	TRY
46	I MISS WHAT WE NEVER HAD	99	WALK WITH ME
		100	WHEN YOU DANCE WITH ME
48	I REGRET NOTHING		
50	I SENT YOU FLOWERS TODAY	101	WHIRLWIND OF SMILES
		103	WINE WILL TELL
52	IF	104	WORK
54	LAMENTS	106	YOU CAME BACK
56	LET ME BE	108	YOU LEAN IN
58	LINES		

ABOUT THE BOOK

You should write what you know. I know emotions. As someone who is fueled by emotions, I have used them to propel me forward on the football field when I needed to dig deep and find a little bit extra. If I played football with you, or against you, lack of intensity is not going to be something that you are going to accuse me of. Football for me is much like life, you have to give it your all.

Off the field, I also profess to being a hot blooded and passionate person. I got my inspiration to write from life experiences. Some were tough to deal with and writing allowed me a cathartic outlet to channel my thoughts. At first the catharsis was self-serving, as it allowed for all the pent-up frustrations of dealing with external forces beyond my control. As I started to be more introspective and examined my life, it became apparent that the reason that I needed to write was to keep writing because I had so much to share. It made me feel good.

I don't apologize for what I write or the way that I write it. Some might say that my style is very direct, raw, and intense. In my opinion, that is what life is, in your face, unapologetic and powerful. Life is random, fragile, short, and yet ever so beautiful. The recent loss of two amazing friends in my life made me realize that I am not going to leave things unsaid, unwritten and undone.

I tend to see the human condition through a series of experiences that we all share, such as love, loss, friendship, relationships, children, parents, family, pain, rage, kindness, generosity, attention, dedication, service and extremely hard work. The hundreds of hours that I have invested in this book have been that of love.

It is ok to say that we love. It is what makes us so wonderfully passionate.

We are able to conceptualize abstract thoughts and convey them in a way that creates a unique experience. I hope that when you read it, you can escape into or from your thoughts, and allow yourself to feel. Feel the word-pictures that I paint and remember, dream, feel those feelings which may lay dormant and have not been accessed in a very long time.

Some people go through life without ever feeling a kiss, a caress, a warm hug, and the love of another human being. I want this book to be that warm hug for people to experience. It is ok to laugh, cry and everything in between when you read poetry. It is your experience. If even one poem in this book makes you think or feel something wonderful, then I feel (as a writer), I have accomplished my goal.

Read all the poems one after the other, or go to titles that intrigue you first! The experience is yours. I hope that you can relate to some of your own life experiences from the words and rhymes, or perhaps that of others in your life. Perhaps the waves of thoughts and feelings will pick you up, and lift you into a wondrous place where you will say to someone in your life who matters an awful lot: Eye Love you.

WORDS OF THANKS

The list of people who have played a role in the creation of this book are numerous and therefore impossible to do justice to thank them individually. To do so, I would have to write a separate book just to do that. Instead of thanking you all one at a time, I am going to tell you how your support contributed.

To my friends and family, who received poems to review and give feedback on, you have guided this otherwise chaotic artistic mindset of mine to give direction, including some of your life experiences which I turned into a narrative poem. If you recognize yourself in a poem, do not be surprised. I have infused what I know and feel into the work. Little by little, I harnessed my emotions, whether it was sadness, joy, anger, pain, gratefulness, happiness, and made them work for me. Most often than not, poems would come rushing out over a ten-minute period of inspiration. Thank you for giving me honest and at times critical feedback about my writing. At times, I applied your suggestions and at times I rationalized why I wanted the verse to sound exactly like that and left it alone. To all of you who have said that my poems moved you or made you cry and reflect, I took that to heart and made a note immediately. Thank you.

I want to thank Marsha Robinson and Marc Klaamas for their hard work on the cover, and for the donation of pictures for this project. Your infinite patience and professionalism on this project was invaluable. Your eye for detail and suggestions, as well as your technical know-how have made the cover exactly as I envisioned it. I would like to acknowledge Adrienne Dier, another photographer whose pictures were used in the book. You have a great eye for composition and detail. A thanks to Pierre-Paul Huet for his pictures and support as well early on with the book. Lastly, Jason Matthews, my longtime friend and quill wielder, thank you for your suggestions, clever editing, suggestions and support throughout the entire process. Can't wait to read your book!

Thank you to everyone at FriesenPress for your work at making this book take physical shape. Paul Fitzgerald from Salt & Pepper Media inc, you are a great publicist and I am thankful for knowing you, having you in my corner and bringing this book alive.

Andrew and Kyle, my boys, you have been my most amazing muses, supporters and cheering section that I could have ever asked for. You put up with me when I told you that I had to put things on pause during an activity, pull over to the side of the road to jot down an idea, or to spend an hour at a time writing. I try to be the best dad possible and do my utmost at all times, and like I taught you, that is all that I ask from you. The pursuit of doing better when we know that we can do better is more the goal than achieving better. Do your best at all times. It is as simple as that. Some days your best might be little, some days your best might be a lot. You will know what you are capable of doing.

I can't wait to see how you both do! It might be a tall order, but I know that you are going to rise to the challenges that you are going to face in your lives with the same grit and tenacity that you possess and have shown when times have been tough.

Know that you are enough, have always been enough and will always be enough in my eyes, and that I love you 100%.

Charlie

AS WE SLEEP

This woman of beauty, both inner and out,
Lays her head next to me without a single doubt.
She pulls me close to her, heaving breasts covered in lace,
Kisses me softly, then lays her hand on my face.

Moonlight covers her in a soft blanket of grey,
Her breathing rhythmic and steady as she lays.
Just a few minutes ago her laughter was loud,
Now her nuzzled mouth betrays a smile that is proud.

Her story is long with many turns, some up and some down,
It makes one wonder where she finds her beautiful crown.
Does she sleep peacefully, dreams of white doves within?
Or do dark larks of pain hatch from her alabaster skin?

She is angelic as she sleeps next to me,
I am happy to have met her and I hope so is she.
The room is motionless except for her gentle sway,
Each time she stirs, she nuzzles closer to me.

I can't see her thoughts, her wants or her tears,
All I can do is hold her close as she dreams.
My eyes grow heavy, as my own dreams are near,
With her beside me there is nothing I fear.

With legs entangled in the middle of the night,
We know the other is there and that all things are right.
We both are unsure of what tomorrow will hold,
So we hold on to each other like birds in the cold.

BETTER OR BITTER

We always have a choice to make
It's not easy to choose at the fork
To keep things real or act a fake
To be the cool one or the dork

When we decide on matters huge
It comes down to our own choice
Love yourself to not move in circles
Make them hear your inner voice

Time to choose the path to take
And one to certainly avoid
Allow some time to not react
And for certain don't look annoyed

One path leads to solitude
The other to untold riches
Drive your car with care
So to avoid treacherous ditches

Your relationship never stays static
It shrinks or it grows by leaps
Don't pile your experiences together
But love them and play for keeps

Don't hold back the love for yourself
Allow the deep feelings to flow
With a great deal of meditation
The answer will be a yes or a no.

You either get bitter and shut down
Withdraw and close the curtains again
Or bring on the smiles and the progress
And become peacefully happy like Zen.

BREAKFAST IN BED

The sweet aroma of roasted coffee
Mingles with that of bacon and eggs
Fragrant pancakes with whipped cream
Serve it up before it grows legs.

She coos when you open the door
Food on a tray that is steady
Eyes open and a smile appears
Someone's tummy must be ready.

The coffee's aroma hits her nose
She throws off the covers and smiles
He just made her whole month with
The simple fact that he tries.

The bacon and eggs dance on her fork
Then disappear behind chewing teeth
Pancakes follow and whipped cream
She tries not to inhale it all...it's a feat.

Smiles and kisses are your payment
And in your ear, she whispers her plans
You take the trey away once empty,
Return to your love and take her hands.

Gently touching her as she loves to be
Caressed and kissed incessantly
You continue making her morning
An unforgettable experience truly.

You love each other and show just that
Not just with words but action instead
Best way to get and remain so close
Is to have breakfast together in bed.

BRIDGE TO THE WILLOW TREE

You grew up in a different way
Far from hands that held you tight
You looked for safety in other ways
Arms of people who were not right.

A patchwork of relationships
Lay in the froth of your life's wake
None of them covered the holes
That each failure left in haste.

You look in the mirror at times
Remembering the person there
Not seeing the beauty as I do
No one close to breathe your air.

They may be kind and funny
But they don't meet the mark
When you stay too long it hurts
Then you are left alone in the dark.

The loneliness is crippling at times
As are the tears that always come
Not showing who you really are
Is a familiar barrier to overcome.

The wall which you have built up
Stands tall, wide and strong
Keeps out all that would approach
No matter their beautiful song.

It is time to take some of the bricks
From that strong and useful wall
And begin to build a bridge to love
Steady, powerful and tall.

Step onto the bridge and smile
For the first one is always hard
Don't let your fear paralyze you
Let down your shield, your guard.

Your beauty and grace are evident
The sense of style easy to see
The image which you created
Is like a solid old oak tree.

In the wind it is inflexible
Leaves catch sail and branches break
To rebuild it is impossible
The broken branches in the lake.

Be like the supple willow tree
Its beauty lies within the sway
As the wind blows it moves
No branches breaking away.

Your beauty shines from within
And matches the one I see
Believe me when I tell you
That you alone hold the key.

Put on your best smile and shoes
Take a deep breath and be free
Find love and someone worthy
Cross the bridge to the willow tree.

BROKE AND BROKEN

As we go through life and toil
Discern the facts from fakes
The reality sets in for most only
After they cut the wedding cake.

The quirks you thought were oh so cute
Begin to drive an awful wedge
Push you two apart until
You both fall off the ledge.

You lose your home, your money
They get their pound of flesh
Much like a spider after a storm
One has to start off building fresh.

You are not sure who you really are
So through many fails and tries
Meeting people not right for you
Hoping not for the goodbyes.

Stress is murder, much like crows
Which bill should you pay
Only way to get ahead
Is through a clever new way.

Reinventing all that was you
While keeping all the good
You shake with fear of not being
Good enough as you should.

You stretch your budget weekly
Making sure that kids get fed
Allowing for time to breathe deep
And for all to get ahead.

Money is tight but air is free
So take a deep breath and go
From one task to another, then
You will have more to show.

As pressure diminishes slowly
You will see the light. You will!
To juggle all expectations
Becomes a daily skill.

You look for small positives
In both written word or spoken
This too shall pass pretty soon
You are just broke and broken.

CHRISTMAS ALONE

I stare at the beautiful Christmas tree
As the lights reflect off silver balls
The shimmering waves of red and white
Distract from the empty green walls.

Another holiday spent drink in hand
Trying to forget that you are free
No one to hang out with and cuddle
Nor to share the egg nog with glee.

Reminiscing about past Christmases
Family is far, they call and wish me well
When the phone rings I smile a bit
They send their love, which is swell.

Is it a curse or some sordid chance
For with each Christmas it appears
That subtle lights of smiling loneliness
Floods my heart while I wipe my tears.

The night air so crisp and cold
Takes my breath away as I slowly walk
Stars accompany my every step
Without a single word; I don't talk.

The snow fall gives sign that its coming.
It feels less foreign every year
That I will not see a paired Holiday
As the season grows so very near.

Perhaps the stars will align one day
And my luck will change and then
No longer will I have Christmas alone
But rather love will live in my pen.

CHRISTMAS LOVE

It's Christmas again, and the snow falls
White blanket reflects the bright light
From a full moon that shines warmly
We are celebrating with love tonight.

As I glance out my frosted window
I see the familiar car pulling up
She gets out and heads to the back end
Pops the trunk while I sip my cup.

I hurry to give her a hand with it all
With shiny bags, or wondrous things
Most of them wrapped with great care,
Decorated with gold and silver strings.

She puts her handful on the counter
I do the same, and then like a script,
We embrace like long lost magnets
Natural longing replaced with bliss.

We make egg nog, with spiced rum
Start to cook a savory, festive meal
Smiles and jokes lighten the mood
The food fragrant and the bliss is real.

The cleanup is quick as we both do
What needs to be done as a team
We sit in front of the fireplace
Snuggle tightly, hold hands as we dream.

The tree reflects the lights within
On the top branch sits a white dove
From both of our hearts oozes
Happiness and Christmas Love.

DEEP

You are not the type to let stuff go
For it all has some meaning to you
Have to figure out the reasons
Behind simple words if they are true.

Harsh words seldom pass you by
Without leaving a burning gash
On the surface of your soul
With love you scratch the rash.

Each heartbreak takes its ugly toll
Piece of your heart you give away
When playing games with others
You must always "fairly" play.

The depth of your soul is an abyss
Reaching sunlight is rare at best
When you bask in the light you realize
That you belong in the quiet depths.

The way others play with your feelings
Tends to become tiresome and mean
As you give of yourself freely
You both become brilliant and clean.

At night when you lay your head down
Try to breathe softly and drift to sleep
Imagine a world full of empaths
Where everyone is strong and deep.

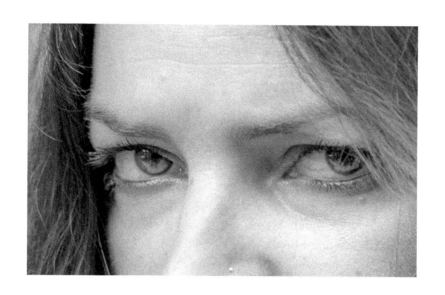

DON'T ENVY OUR LOVE

We listen to you talk of beautiful themes
Idealized relationship that you construct hyper-fast.
You see the harvest of amber fields of grain
Not the hard work which made the fields last.

We wake up early and think of the other
Make their coffee just the way they like it.
Wake them up gently with thoughts of joy
To reflect in the touches as they feel it.

How we say I love you is like yours perhaps
There are many ways to say it so they feel good.
I believe in you! You matter to me! How was your day?
Wear your coat it's cold outside! Want to share my food?

When feelings are hurt, we talk it out
Don't let things fester until it blows.
On the other hand, we let little things
Go by the wayside until the moon brightly glows.

At times, there are huge obstacles
That test our love...that's true.
We forgive quickly and find a reason
To be happy together and not blue.

Get to work, no time to waste on minutia
Think of ways to unite rather than to part.
Don't envy our love as it is a result
Of inspiration plus perspiration; it's an art.

Look inside your partner's soul
And find what pulls you together.
Don't envy our love…for it is ours
Yours is yours, if you just hold on forever.

DRAGON

I feel the pain that sears my brain
Each time I think about me and you
Every deep breath burns my lungs
And sharply sears my throat too.

The lingering thoughts of sadness
Gain momentum in my head
They rock back and forth
And I wish that I was dead.

The place of peace and serenity
Only a distant place in time
I dare not look for helping hands
For they might hasten mine.

The sweet smell of strong elixirs
Call me to fly to them again
To release the dragon so it can feed
On my pain and numb my brain.

I make excuses and wreck the streak
Climb in the bottle with salty tears
Knowing that I can't control it
And it has hold of all my fears.

The dragon devours all my hard work
With great talons it holds my heart
As it gains strength and power steadily
All logic and reason fall apart.

I watch it feeding in the mirror
Powerless I stand there frozen
One fevered bite after another
May as well be my blood again.

Drink goes in and pain goes out
Its belly getting full and tight
The creature tightens its grip on me
Its reflection prepares for flight.

We become one and the lines blur
Where one starts and the other ends
No need to hold back tears or feelings
We pushed away all of our friends.

We battle each other through the night
Hate and love incessantly collide
The price of life is servitude
The dragon never leaves my side.

Exhausted we lay like empty vessels
Each time the result a bloody draw
It goes to sleep to be awakened
When the chains are cut by a pain-saw.

The dragon sleeps within me
Lurking and keeping an open eye
It will never leave my mind
No matter how hard I try.

Oceans of people who have dragons too
They might not be made of booze
They struggle with their own demons
Or creatures who they do not choose.

I speak my truth so you see beyond
My shell, down to my hidden gears
Never think that you are alone
The dragon feeds on your fears.

One day when life doesn't hurt as much
The dragon will work with me
To keep the painful thoughts in check
And will sleep beneath the sea.

EYE LOVE YOU

I can't form the words to say
The things I feel for you,
So I will attempt to write them
A few verses...that I can do.

You came into my life with zeal
Like a whirlwind, you stole my heart,
Knowing you are next to me
There is nothing I can't start.

You brought such joy, marvelous light
That shines on everything we do,
It touches lives in the best ways
And it propels us both anew.

I see you are getting better
At tasks you thought were tough,
Battling through all obstacles
Work hard and know you're enough.

You are enough for me. Always were
Your worth is not always visible,
The sheer power you have within
Is absolutely radiant, and incredible.

There are words that encourage
And others that make you feel,
The power in your thoughts and deeds
Hold more than only visual appeal.

We tend to see the world today
With eyes that judge and hurt,
Ourselves or other people
No matter what their worth.

Know this my dear: You are perfect
You have qualities through and through,
I close my eyes and see you smile
But above else.....Eye Love You.

FATHER OR DAD

Most men can be fathers
Some of them are dads
Dads don't take the easy road
And leave as if they were fads.

Dads stick around and raise you
With a hand that's gentle and strong
They never let you go a second without
Showing you love and that you belong.

Dads encourage other fathers
To do better than their own
Act bravely and not to hide tears
Torn clothing can be sewn.

A father is a family member
They fulfill a certain role
A Dad is someone who oozes love
And teaches you as he grows old.

There are no written guidelines
Nor a magic all-encompassing list
To be the dad your kids will respect
And to seek you out if they are pissed.

If you have a choice to be one
I suggest you choose to be a Dad
For there are already enough fathers
Who can't grow and love...it's sad.
I Love You Dad.

FLOWER THAT I LOVED

We shared a long salty afternoon
The drinks flowed like waterfalls
We barely paused to take a breath
It ended in vaudevillian pratfalls.

The phones echoed our calls at night
Like two deep cavernous holes
Both of us wanting to fit in
No matter how different the souls.

So try we did, for a little while
The surface was like mirrors
Reflecting the beauty, but hiding the truth
That we were both driven by different fervors.

You said that there were limits
Of how much you could give me
However, capacity for love was one thing
That leads to longevity.

I thought you were not far away
You shut the door and that finished me up
Promises of friendship evaporated instantly
Like water from a shattered cup.

Did I fail to hear your silent plea?
Which screamed out loudly "Let me go!"
I picked the flower that I loved
Instead I should have let you grow.

FORK IN THE ROAD

The road ahead is tough enough
Without the need to choose
Which way will you win the most?
And which way will you surely lose?

When you face the fork in the road
Must decide to go ahead
Weigh your options before the choice
Put your worrying to bed.

One choice is going to lead you down
A road you never dreamed of
The other just as marvelous as
The first but one you could have...

If you take one road and not the other
Don't look back, go full steam ahead
Impossible to split yourself in two
So put the "What if's" to bed.

We make hundreds of choices per day
One of them is our approach, attitude
A positive one can help you take flight
And determine your altitude.

The time has come to sink or swim
You know exactly what to do
Take the first step and suddenly
The fork in the road is behind you.

FRIENDS FIRST

There is no rush to change it
No reason to upset the cart
You like each other, show it
Don't let pressure push you apart.

You have met and want to see if
You can laugh and sing and play
See the other's character
Behind the curtain as you pull it away.

When you know that they are worthy
They have a brain, a heart and some wit
Take a chance to go further
Leap forth and just go with it.

The friendship will surely ground you
The romance will take away your breath
Don't compare each other to past ones
New relationships are the best.

Hold hands in the park as you saunter
Feed birds like on an old movie screen
Just go with your gut feeling
This person says what they mean.

Those times when you will disagree
Respectfully talk do not shout
You don't have to take it to heart
Though it's ok to take a self-timeout.

You both will come to a garden
Where the time will surely show
The right path, perhaps a love story
Out of your garden passion will grow.

Love your friend and love your partner
Don't let caution quench your thirst
Allow your heart to guide you and
Make sure that you are friends first.

GONE

The way we met was through a joke...
She laughed and I did too.
The reason why we liked each other
Neither one of us knew.

There has to be no reason
Why two people fall in like.
As we grew closer the nights got colder
Enough for a match to strike.

You told me things and I shared too
My fears and oh the dreams.
It only took a moment
To turn giggles into screams.

As quickly as you appeared
A speck in time as whole.
There is an empty space here now
My heart paid a heavy toll.

I miss you already, hugs and kisses
The smiles and fun we shared.
For a moment, I was happy again
We tried and yes, we dared.

Our paths have crossed and I wish you well
Hope for you nothing but the best.
I will miss your smile, your hugs and all
The secrets, between us rest.

One day when we are old and grey
We might run into each other as we rust.
Will you smile and hug me then my dear
Before we turn to dust?

GOOD MORNING TEXT

The words are simple and direct
They greet you as you wake
Wishing you a good morning
Yet not claiming their stake.

A simple gesture to show thought
Allows you to feel smitten
That you are the first person they
Thought of after their eyes were open.

Do you answer them right away?
Or wait for a few minutes to go by?
It feels good to get words as nice
The best part is that they try.

You make a note for tomorrow
To wish them good morning in turn
They are going to feel fantastic
Just like you did today and you learned.

No need to read too much into it
They might not be head over heels
But it surely counts for something
By how nice it truly feels.

Your feelings for one another quickens
The thought of distance must go
Flirtatious friendship then romance
From closeness, true love will grow.

One day the texts might stop
And something else will take their place
A touch of your hands with theirs
Or a kiss on your nose, lips, and face.

HAND TO HOLD

There once was a woman who was alone as she cried
Strangers became family and the years multiplied
Her beginnings were hard but love held her up
Mid-life brought love in the form of a girl and a pup.

Happiest memories were that with her mother
Hoping for better for herself and for others
Her smile glows as she hopes for love in her life
She had enough of this hard thing called strife.

Ready for love she is, so she takes another chance
To make her life sparkle, to laugh, walk and to dance
A new person to trust and a new hand to hold
The old adage goes that chance favors the bold.

So, she took one more chance on a man with a grin
Laughing together as the loss became a win
He took her hand and he asked her to once again trust
To dance together in the rain and to kick off the rust.

They wanted their lives to have meaning together
When she was cold he would offer his sweater
She took care of him when he was sick, tired or ill
Giving and receiving was the bond that stood still.

She laughs with abandon and holds her head to the sky
Replaces the tears shed with tremendous smiles
She takes his hand, walks, then looks at him more
Happiness has come to walk with her from the shore.

HER EYES

She looks at you with those big eyes
And your world quickly falls apart
Losing all concentration off your task
When your gazes do not depart.

They can catch you at your worst
Build you up when you feel strain
Injecting a desire for calm passion
And taking away all your pain.

A single glance can touch you
Down deep where no one sees
When she slowly turns her head
She can bring you to your knees.

Two windows to her soul, which ache
From a lifetime filled with struggles
She pulls you close for butterfly kisses
And disarms you with her snuggles.

You want the truth, then ask for it
Sidestep all the distorted dark lies
When you desire truth above all else
You have to look her in her eyes.

HOLD ON TIGHT

This life is short and full of struggles
Happy times are few you know
If you find a partner who loves you
Hold on tight and don't let go.

When your day is long and dreary
The weather is calling for snow
They remind you to wear a scarf
Hold on tight and don't let go.

Times of loss they hold your hand
While you walk as a pair to and fro
They hug you tightly as you shiver
Hold on tight and don't let go.

The birthday present is amazing
It actually stopped the show
When thought becomes action
Hold on tight and don't let go.

You dance the night away together
Sway to the music oh so slow
You lock eyes and then lips too
Hold on tight and don't let go.

They are laying in a hospital bed
Will they get better you don't know
Remember all the good times
Hold on tight and don't let go.

Skating together on a frozen canal
Hand in hand you push off your toe
Steady rhythm and patient form
Hold on tight and don't let go.

The trip is long and you miss them a lot
It seems to go so awfully slow
In your mind they are right next to you
Hold on tight and don't let go.

The years pass and you both get older
Like two lobsters don't you know
Claw in claw you fight the currents
Hold on tight and don't let go.

Hold on tight and don't let go.

Hold on tight...

And...

Don't...

Let...

Go!

HOPE

Alone again for the holidays
Most people don't think much of it
They don't remember how it can feel
But you see couples coo and together sit.

Thoughts of soft caresses
And tightly held strong hands
Dance with abandon in your head
Like possible circumstances.

The cold crisp air surges
And in your face blows
You shut your eyes quickly
To protect them from blowing snows.

When you open them you see
A beautiful soul on a bench near by
You approach them and say hello
They smile at you while still shy.

The touch of their kindness
Is only matched with their smarts
Once again the fire inside you
And it opens both your hearts.

Talk and laughter, you both try
To hold back your hopeful way
They don't seem to work out for long
And they never ever stay.

Yet you lace up your skates and
Timidly leave the safety of the bench
Both of you give it a whirl and then
It loosens your heart like a wrench.

You both fall down in turn
And help each other rise
The fear grows into trust
To both people's surprise.

A cup of hot chocolate
Then a stroll in the snow
A simple yet elegant way
To let each other know.

That there are feelings afoot
Which want so badly to grow
In your thawing heart's recesses
Which were frozen just hours ago.

The playful gazes and grins
Become synchronized and glue
Two strangers together
And revitalizes both anew.

Snowballs fly at one another
During escalating giggles
Ends in an embrace out of which
Neither of you wiggles.

With pounding hearts and quickened breath
You pull them close for something more
Your eyes meet; you have no chance
They kiss you like no one has before.

Crescendo of feelings, shared slow kisses
Betray your longing for lore
You don't want to let go of the idea
You hope deep down in your core.

HUGS AND KISSES

As we wait yet again to see each other,
The feelings build and arise.
How nice it is to wrap my arms around
This angel who's in my life.

She looks at me with her radiant smile
As arms snake around my shoulders.
They find their mark and raise my heart beat
It feel like I can lift boulders.

I love your lips…

I graze your cheeks with the back of my hands
You close your eyes and coo
We abandon the world outside
And we become one from two.

Soft skin meets hairy chest and then
Our mouths move closer and ever so lightly
Our lips touch and hands interlock
We hold each other ever so tightly.

Come over here….

The lights go out and the clothes fall off
And we explore our bodies deeper.
The fervor and passions grow quickly
Each kiss and hug feels so much sweeter.

Exploring lips find shoulders and necks
Some bites and nibbles feel great.
Scratching nails on backs and legs
Awaken the body as we anticipate.

I want you…

Our bodies remember what to do
Hands calmly recall how to touch.
Cheek to cheek our boundaries fall
Will it be enough or will it be too much?

I slide close to you as you make me squirm
You pull me close and groan with a smile
We grind our bodies until we release
Together as we motionlessly lie.

Shut up and kiss me…

XOXO

I CAN'T LET YOU GO

I thought I saw you earlier today
She looked just like you
As I opened the door for her
My heart missed a beat or two.

I know that you don't care for me
Nor do you think of our time together
My stupid brain seems to be skipping
Like a needle of a record player.

As songs that play in the bookstore
Paralyzed, I sit in the poetry section
I rewind then play our relationship tapes
And wonder if it was all fiction.

I want to shed the memories of you
But this stupid brain of mine is gone
Beyond reason and carries you
Around like a heavy dark stone.

I have tried to move on with my life
Dated, gone out and met others for food
But my head and heart have seemingly
Agreed to keep you around for good.

So I won't try to get rid of you
I will instead let you set up camp
Perhaps one day you will leave on your
Own and send me a letter with a stamp.

I will breathe a little easier
And will smile more don't you know
But until then I will fake it I guess
But today I can't let you go.

I MISS WHAT WE NEVER HAD

We almost were, but then we weren't
Along our journey we have both been burnt.
The light in our eyes that once was bright
Now is blocked out by eyelids closed so tight.

We almost held hands, and never let go
Like two links of a chain forged and cooled in the snow.
Our hands heavy with work, minds cluttered with tasks
I am too busy, we said when someone would ask.

We almost kissed softly til we both nearly fell...
For each other the feelings were not hard to tell.
Our lips say the words but our bodies just froze
Shivers of attraction zigzagged from our head to our toes.

We almost dated and spent time laughing til dawn
No one anticipates a rook, bishop or pawn.
Like intricate details of a sculpted piece
Unseen is the move which causes the release.

We almost lived as one with our families together
Knowing real well that our love will last at least forever
About the time we never moved in a house
Well beyond the horizon was this game of cat and mouse.

We almost loved each other but the timing was wrong
Peace we could not find even in the best love song.
In moments of clarity I still see us here,
Laughing, loving, kissing, living without fear.

I REGRET NOTHING

I don't regret the day we met
You looked angelic by moonlight
The stars were shining in the dark
Reflecting off your eyes so bright.

I don't regret that I liked your mind
Fell for you the moment you spoke
I would have written a lifetime's worth
Of poems with my pen til it broke.

I don't regret the kisses shared
The nights of passion and lust
The dances we danced til exhaustion
We were fantastic at kicking up dust.

I don't regret the countless jokes
Together we were tickled pink
Laughing until our sides hurt
We were almost oblivious I think.

I don't regret the awkward pauses
The silent moments as they grew
The wedge between us spread apart
All the things we built and knew

I don't regret the time we spent
Uncertain of what we would face
The light has fled from our eyes
And sadness took its place.

I don't regret as you pulled away,
As you gave up on us so fast
But I don't understand the reason
You went silent and I was aghast.

I don't regret the sweet memories
Which we made just you and me
What I do regret is that it is over
And that we will never be.

I SENT YOU FLOWERS TODAY

I decided to send you flowers
Not for the reasons you might think
I knew your favorite color is red
But I asked them to add white and pink.

The red roses and white carnations
Show my thoughts and also my feelings
The red ones ooze deep seeded passion
The white ones...pure joy of giving.

Pink has a special place in my heart
It brings softness to all who can see
The difference in shade and darkness
Which make the pallet delicious to me.

The vase is a great reminder for when
The flowers have all withered and gone
That there is someone who loves you
And will talk with you until dawn.

You will say that I "shouldn't have"
But Baby you know that it is real
Not afraid to tell you the reasons
It is an extension of how I feel.

Appreciate their transient beauty
For life is like a bouquet as well
We all wither like flowers in the end
So with tears water us Ma Belle.

Your smile is the ultimate payment
The laughs and the hugs the change
The great thing about flowers is that
They cover an extensive range.

The note says it all... so keep it
In a place that you soon won't forget
Glance at it sometimes when you feel
The need to feel my love as you fret.

My dear, my darling, my sweetheart,
No other name I can recall or say
Remember that I truly love you when
You see that I sent you flowers today.

IF

If I said that you were marvelous
It would be the understatement of my life
Frightening you away is not my aim
But I would love it if you were my wife.

If you felt the power of my love
Your grip on it would be tight
It would envelope you like a blanket
And make you feel safe like a night light.

If you went away to a foreign land
And left me behind to stay and wait
I wouldn't sleep a single night
Until you walked through the gate.

If you spent an hour in my head
You would understand me well
You would weep from all the beauty...
I see but with words I cannot tell.

If I say nothing and sit next to you
Hold your hand and look like a fool
Not sharing what I think because
I don't want you to think I'm a tool.

I won't bore you with any more thoughts
Which race around my brain
I want to sit together, talk on a bench
And dance in the pouring rain.

If the day turns into a starry night
And we are sitting knee to knee
We gaze up into the deep void
Hold hands, say "So glad you're with me."

LAMENTS

I know that my heart will be whole on a not so distant day.
I know that I will love and be loved by someone worthy.
I know that the dark cloud of despair will dissipate soon.
I know that there is a light at the end of this lifelong hail storm
of emptiness.

Can't feel the words of encouragement through my shield
of solitude.
Can't feel my friends and family's love and their out-
reached hands.
Can't feel anything that is not directly related to my sur-
vival today.
Can't feel the warmth of the sun as it bears down upon me like
a weight.

Don't want to hear the news, as it reminds me of horrific deeds
of men.
Don't want to argue over various beliefs which boil down to the
same rhetoric.
Don't want to chase a dream that seems unattainable.
Don't want to forget those who occupy my heart and
my memories

It hurts when I inhale and my chest feels like it is going to burst.
It hurts to know that you have left.
It hurts even though I attempt to piece it back together daily.
It hurts that loneliness is my life partner.

I hope that love will ultimately carve a place on my tree of life and stay.
I hope that my friends and family remain in my life til the end of my days.
I hope that we all learn a little humility through our life journeys.
I hope that light replaces darkness in our lives.

I dream about galaxies and nebulae and star systems and their majesty.
I dream that I will see you again.
I dream of days filled with laugher, pleasures and fun times.
I dream of sitting on a porch swing with you until way past sunset.

LET ME BE

Leave my thoughts and don't come back
All you cause me is heartache and strife
We would both be better off if you left
Without a single piece of you in my life.

Take your selfish vagabond ways
And enjoy the windy road ahead
I couldn't give you what you wanted
Hope you find someone new instead.

I wish that we had never met
Cause I loved you, I truly did
Too bad that whatever we shared
Was wasted time...I was so stupid.

You want to stay friends, as you smile
As if nothing happened...why?
I have already moved on from you
And want to see you just to wave bye.

To tell the truth you never leaned in
All you needed was a pastime
Too bad you couldn't open your heart
Instead you just played with mine.

Unfeeling cold emotionless mess
You are truly unable to cry
If you allowed yourself to feel again
You'd crumble like a cracker that's dry.

Don't want your friendship, be gone!
It's not an order or a decree
Do me a favor and please get lost
You can just disappear and let me be!

LINES

This one I got when I howled so loud
After a joke that made me laugh
I slapped my knee as I bent over
I was so happy I folded in half.

The ones around my eyes appeared
When I saw my children be born
They were the result of continuous smiles
Which were chains never ever torn.

My mouth is adorned with tons of them
As I was surprised by many acts
The reality is that they are "feeling badges"
Unchained freedoms and disguised facts.

You see my face which is imperfect now
Ravaged by unfeeling claws of time
Can you see the young person there
Who was attractive in their prime?

I look in the mirror and what do I see
Is it me of yesterday?
Or is it a soul all withered and old
Like a dried-up leaf which is grey?

This one right here, the one I just got
Was from the love that I still feel
For all those people in my life
Who next to me stood like steel.

Their love for me and worried frowns
Translate from hearts full of love
They showed me kindness and patience
Never feel that they are above.

We pay for choices good or bad
Sometimes payments come in fines
The strong feelings are etched
On our faces forever in form of lines.

LONG TO BELONG

Rushing through the day's work
Just to make it home.
Seeking parity with someone special
But who is not your clone.

They do the same and hurry up
As they drive with extra care
When they get through the door
The cupboards are never bare.

A kind word and a smile
Show that we care more than most.
That care can take on many forms
Sometimes it is tea and others it's toast.

Hug each other, carry on
Through many daily tasks.
It feels like heaven when
You give them something before they ask.

The ties that hold it all together
Are love, respect, kindness and passion.
Not the traps of money, power
Or the lords and ladies of fashion.

We like to be side by side
Hip to hip like a great team.
We long to belong to one another
And we work hard at our dream.

LOVE LOVE!

Do not recoil when they say that they do
Nor when it's given honestly with trust
Allow the feeling to resonate within
Do not mistake it for only bare lust.
Love Love!

This feeling that you circumvent
Cause it has steered you wrong so oft,
Might lead you down a path of dreams
And make your hard ticker feel soft.
Love Love!

Are the words real or are they mush?
There is only one way to find out.
Return them with equal softness
Do not recoil quickly or simply pout.
Love Love!

Let those who profess to know just be
Loud and share brightly coloured boasts
Examine all depth of your own thoughts
And love back stronger than most.
Love Love!

Love is strange as it doesn't feel
It takes a heart to give it life
The only thing extinguishes its flame
Is another's thrust with a dull knife.
Love Love!

Let it flow like wine from a shared cup
And soak through your soul like a sieve
Imbibe the frothy sweetness as
You learn again how to live.
Love Love!

Love is a feeling, a concept, a thing
That deals us a hand which is wild
Play the person and not the hand
With a heart as pure as that of a child.
Love Love!

You are no longer alone and afraid
When you become friends with love
Like a tabby cat hugging its friend
The white-tailed cooing dove.
Love Love!

Love Love my darling it loves you as well
Be brave and daring no matter the tides
Love Love with all your might in the end
Til Love's Love in you happily resides.
Love Love!

LOVE NOTES

Your words and actions are a gift to me
The things you do are ever so sweet
There is no one who makes me feel
The way you show me love is a treat.

Little notes you leave for me
In my clothes, my bag, my lunch
I read them and think of you
And how I like you a bunch.

I wake up, then I go make coffee
In the can there is a scribble
"Thanks for making me my drink"
Which I take to you without a dribble.

I get my coat on, shoes and hat
A note falls out entitled "My Dear…"
I pick it up and grin as I read:
"I love you, miss you already it's clear!"

As I go to pay the bridge toll I find
A few lines in my wallet that say
"Thank you for working so hard for us"
I smile as I roll my window down and pay.

Supper is over and we do the dishes
The load is lighter for two it's true
The last note of the day is under a plate
"Meet me in the bedroom in two!"

LOVE OF A LIFETIME

Empty promises and broken dreams
Line the inside of your heart
Never having that forever-peace
A lover to play that special part.

You take the leap of faith again
Put yourself out to hang and dry
They seem like they might understand
The reason you always try.

Both believe in the power of love
But will wait for it if need be
Settling for less is not in the cards
Nor is rushing in blindly.

You take your time and pause a while
It is actually tremendously hard to do
But sweet, sweet timing is always
The most important to both of you.

If they truly see your worth, they
Ease your pain and dry your tears
With brave steady steps you both
Walk hand in hand without fears.

Fears that used to cripple you
Now fall quickly to the wayside
As you come up to them you see
Your own strength blossom from inside.

Reflections of self in a partner's gaze
Tell you more than what you can bare
So you close your eyes when up close
Anticipating a kiss if you dare.

They complete you in every way
And so you are smiling my dear
Let love develop in that manner
And fight together the demons of fear.

The journey can seem perilous
Together the load is lighter
Adoring glances from a partner
Softens the most ardent fighter.

A lovely, flirtatious, light hearted kiss
Lifts your spirits as if you could fly
Tremendous winds beneath you
Carry you around as you try, try and try.

From empty promises that break you
To surprising ones that last
Uproot your knowledge of people
Leave the lies peacefully in the past.

Holding hands through stormy nights
Spooning so close together is a gift
Tethers of your heart intertwine and
From each other you never drift.

LULLABY FOR WOLVES

The cold wind howls through the night
As the pack circles up to eat
When you are hungry you have to kill
And that's not an easy feat.

To tear the flesh from a creature
Small, fast, big or quick
What makes it hard is that if you miss
You grow weak and get sick.

Exhausted they lay in their den
With bellies full of prey
Hunting elk took a heavy toll
Two of them wounded lay.

Heavy panting and rhythmic breaths
Are all that you can audibly hear
The grey one howls repeatedly
Music to a wolf's tired ears.

Fighting the urge to sleep is hard
Like ignoring a bell that tolls
The howling of wind and of kin
Is like a lullaby for wolves.

MEAL FOR ONE

The waitress brings the menu
And the look she gives you know
"Will you wait for your party
To order?" The answer is a "No".

You read the paper, play on your phone
Time is your ally and friend
No matter how many look at you
There is nothing to explain or defend.

Happy you are, spending time with you
Your bestie is in the mirror for certain
Enjoy the time that is allotted you
As any time it could be curtains.

The hot food comes, and loudly sizzles
Enticing sound, smell and sight
Prior to devouring the whole thing
You give thanks for being able to fight.

Each morsel passes your lips as in a film
Have to slow down to savor it all
Choosing where your next meal will be
Only on your shoulders it does fall.

Meal time with friends and family
Many arguments can be lost or won
Doesn't beat the silence and peace
That offers a meal for one.

MISS THE GIFTS

I am not much for trinkets or shiny things
A warm hug would be better spent
The notion of having someone care
And to help you set up a camping tent.

The lights all shine in the snow
Couples walk hand in hand.
You recall with a smile when you
Did the same barefoot in the sand.

Holidays come and birthdays do too
You long for times of laughter
How wonderful it would be to share
And to belong to another for ever after.

It's not the gifts that make it great
But the thoughtful gestures that show
Someone has made space in their heart
Thought of you and wants you to know.

Exchanging gifts is a simple act
We do it daily without thought
Strengthening the human bonds
Relationships sail and are hard-fought.

At times the links can become brittle
The chain is strengthened by gifts
Reinforcing the weld is the notion
That the act of giving helps us and lifts.

I don't miss the act of receiving things
But rather long for a person with tact
Masquerading as a lightning rod for fun
That's why I miss the gifts... it's the act.

MOTHER LIKE NO OTHER

My mom is special just like yours
She taught me right from wrong
The way I learned to do things right
Is what made me so very strong.

Her words of warning echo loudly
Each time I cross a busy road
It doesn't matter how old I get
I wear my coat in the cold.

Lessons were many through the years
She never stopped to pause
Tirelessly she bandaged me
And at times used lots of gauze.

As kids grow up they leave the home
But you never leave your mother
You may get a partner but never leave
Her heart as there is no other.

A phone call away, yet miles apart
To measure, the distance is too great
Her words of wisdom are heard still
"Love them, there's no reason for hate."

As adults we grow and families form
The daily chores quickly multiply
Sometimes we forget the person
Who gave us wings and helped us to fly.

So if your mother still can hear
Or see or talk or she can listen
Call her up or go and see her
For her you always glisten.

She loves you now as she loved you then
Her love for you just grows and grows
Don't worry if you have been fighting
Her love for you is intact, that she knows.

When your time comes to be old and grey
You will smile and happy you will be
The love you will feel toward your kids
When they call or come, you to see.

Love and mother are synonyms
Mine loves me just like back then
Mother is a word that is like
No other word.....Je t'aime.

I love you MOM

MOTHER'S DAY FUN

I sat there drinking at the coffee shop
My day was free and somewhat slow
I noticed a woman with her son
With laughter, their bond was sure to grow.

She smiled at him and attentively
They sat down and began to play
A game of cards that many of us know
Go Fish was what they'd say.

He wanted to get his own drink so
She gave him money and sent him up
When his drink was ready
They went together to get his cup.

It was not about the card game
Nor about the drink they shared
It was the time they spent together
And she showed him that she cared.

NO CLUE AT ALL

When she was younger it was different
She thought she knew her path
Now, after many trips around the sun
She is unsure where she'll hang her hat.

The benefit of getting older is that
You put it all out there from the start
Hide very little as there is no point
It all comes out in the wash of the heart.

Her friends and family are all hitched
Paired-off in unions of seeming bliss
She longs for a connection; an equal
She no longer is looking for twists.

Happiness comes from within you see
It puts you at ease if you please
She is seeking a partner; fellow traveler
One who makes her smile with ease.

She longs for a lover who gets her
Who doesn't care what others think
To her, intelligence is more than sexy
But not beyond a wonderful wink.

She knows her own mind most of the time
But it can betray her for the now
Her mother told her "You can't make
A golden purse from the ear of a sow."

She is putting herself out there
Taking chances on short or tall
He might be right in front of her
But her heart has no clue at all.

PETRICHOR

The sky is grey with heavy clouds
As the wind picks up the dust
The air is thick with anticipation
A weather change is a must.

She walks with purpose, but suddenly
Her dress is caught by the wind
With steadying hands, she grabs at it,
And stays upright without making a stink.

She slows down her pace and finally stops,
As the gusts die down and pause
There is something familiar here,
She just needs to find the cause.

A memory old and sweet emerges,
And whispers in her ear and trembles…
"Remember the smell of the air before
Rains fell over a camp fire's hot embers!"

The dust kicks up as the rain hits the ground,
Each droplet or water a bomb.
Reminds her of her sweet childhood days
When she used to walk in the rain with mom.

The smile, which has now sat on her face
Makes her feel young and free again.
The smell of falling rain on a fire perhaps
"Petrichor…my favorite word" she thought just then.

POPPY IS HERE

There is no wrinkled hand here
To hold my child's or mine
Remember the price they all paid
It's etched in stone and time.

The sea of red and white is waving
To the lives that it took to pay
Slides and play parks all over
Are filled with free kids who play.

Gramps, or Poppy, is with us still
In the form of laughs and smiles
We speak his name with pride
As our free country's flag flies.

With tearful eyes we remember
"In Flanders Fields" we recite
Gramps is with us as we smile
Poppy is with us again tonight.

RUNNING FROM YOURSELF

The journey starts like many others
With hope and joy and trust
No matter how we guard ourselves
To toughen up is ultimately a must.

We tend to help our fellow neighbors
And the old to cross the streets
No matter how we stretch the blanket
It seldom covers your cold feet.

The times we plow through aimlessly
Mistakes we make more than a ton
Careful planning and trepidation
Seldom produce unforgettable fun.

When the wounds of life become
Too raw and at times even drole
We pull away and turn to run
What's inviting is a dark hole.

The nerves are shot and eyes are too
How much we tend to feel
The once strong heart which beat fiercely
Now resembles anything but steel.

We close the curtains and shut the blinds
Time stands still and we stand stunned
Mountains of endless aching feelings
Away from light we run, then grunt.

The dark grows and we become lost
Can't find our way to any smiles
We try to run from ourselves
And we run for miles and miles.

The longest trek in a person's life
Is to find true happiness within
We think that this can somehow come
If we change physical space again.

As we get tired from constant running
Our energy steadies and quickly fades
If this was school and subjects feelings
We would get steady failing grades.

Your legs get tired and you take
The feelings, place them on a shelf
You run until you have to face them
And stop running from yourself.

SEND THE SAND

You told me that you would keep me
In your thoughts as you fly far
Each beach you visit a vial of sand
You will send to me as a postcard.

Wasn't certain you would keep your word
But they started arriving one by one
A short note accompanying each
Describing your trip and the incessant fun.

They line my top shelf and I glance there often
Cause I know that you thought of me
I wonder if I will ever be free
To one day leave and join you with glee.

Time is passing and the only way
To have news is vials of sand
That accumulate and are seemingly
Taking your place which is grand.

One day the dry sand vials stopped coming
Replaced by ones with wet sand instead
So the thoughts started racing in me
The story I made up, completed, in my head.

Were you crossing beaches or shores?
Or wide deserts with little drink?
Perhaps the wet sand was a clue of sorts
Which I had to figure out and think.

It never really made a lot of sense
That you stopped writing to me
The only thought that never left
Was that one day one another we'll see.

Each month a vial comes and I place it
With the hundred or so other ones
Smiling and hoping that you know
That my heart belongs to you...it does.

Finally free from obligation
I pack my bags and leave to face my fears
As my plane lands I run to find the girl
Who sent me vials through all the years.

I ask around to get direction
If they know where you can be found
They point and smile when I ask
I run toward your house; on your door I pound.

The person who answers the door
Looks strangely like they know me
They guide me to the flower garden
Where I quickly fall to my knees.

You look as beautiful as the day you left
Your smile is bright and sweet
The only difference is that you are missing
One of your arms and both feet.

You tell me that since the accident
You have thought about me
How you wanted to come home
But was scared of how it might be.

The scars of an exploding mine
Were too much for you to share
So you kept sending me your tears
Mixed with sand it was all you could bare.

In reality, your beauty lies within
I want you for good in my life
Your appearance is just the package
Would you love me and be my wife?

I kiss you with eyes full of tears
Showing you my unwavering love
I don't care about what you look like
Your heart is like a white dove.

SHE WAS SURE

Their eyes met on a crowded beach
Shared smiles and then a meal
The laughs that came from their time
Together was more than real.

She compared him to every man
Who has tried to woo her before
He surpassed them in wit and charm
Which sent shivers through her core.

The way he looked at her smiling face
Allowed for flow like hourglass sand
When she glanced down next time
They were sitting there, hand in hand.

"Let's go for a walk" he said to her
The response was surely implied
Both got up after paying the bill
Still linked, began synchronized strides.

They shared a walk on the sandy beach
Chaperoned only by shiny stars
She felt that his words were like music
Healing her heart's numerous scars.

Her laughter made him feel immense
And like no other woman had done,
Her gentleness strengthened his will
To share dreams and refuse to be alone.

The night together turned into a day
Neither wanting an end or a cure
And then that day turned into a lifetime
He loved her...of this she was sure.

STRENGTH FROM TEARS

Happiness is but a remote memory
To the one who cries over foam,
The feeling of never-ending failure
Strengthens the shield; the dome.

Much like a force field from sci-fi
It protects the ones who are within,
Its generation takes kilowatts of power
The animal kingdom has chitin.

Another form of stress relief,
In the shape of salty drops of tears,
When you feel overwhelmed or sad
They flow down your cheeks into beers.

The tears that make puddles at first
Take on a role that they never sought
Peace is the goal... which is hopeful
And battles won after being fought.

As winds pick up and intensify
You must be alert and on edge
A false move and it's a disaster
Access all your skill and knowledge.

The tears travel down your cheeks
Drip on your neck and then depart
To make their way to your chest
And seep into your pounding heart.

So… cry the tears, and know that
It is your heart that they fuel
Allow them to flow freely
No need to be a steadfast fool.

Each drop of sadness grows as if
It wants to go and fill your chest
Strength from tears can help you
To pass tremendously hard tests.

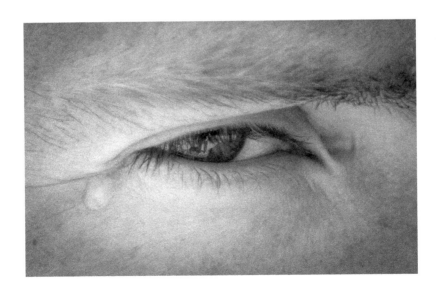

TAKE HER BACK

Her lips trembled but no sound escaped
As she glared at you with wet eyes
What she wanted to say was painful
Though the payoff outweighed lies.

She knew that she had made a mistake
By casting you hastily aside
Only then did she realize
That she wanted to be by your side.

She mustered the courage to talk to you
So you decided to hear her out
No need to get angry or to yell
But most of all you must not pout.

Admire her courage to stand there
To tell you how she really feels
Hear her out and then decide
If your heart can beat as it heals.

She tells you that you were missed
Both day and lonely night
In you she lost a best friend
Leaving her alone with chest tight.

Will you take a chance on her
Are you going to let her crack...
Your armor which you have crafted
From sadness... and take her back?

TEARS OF A CLOWN

I make you laugh night after night
The performance never fails
Create laughter from your tears
My skills often blaze new trails.

The multitude of plays I perform
Pale in comparison to those
That nightly unfurl in my head
Where I wittily disarm my foes.

You never see the sadness
And I seldom share my thoughts
What you see is what I show you
Behind the curtains lay so much.

The laughter that we shared at times
Carries me through to the morn
When I try to close my eyes and sleep
I see monster vines with sharp thorns.

I am a clown and I make you grin
Forget your troubles and woes
My solitude is painful at times
So much so that it turns my nose.

I hold on to this pot of flowers
At least they don't put me down
They get lots of watering
From the sad tears of a clown.

THE FIVE W'S

When we strongly disagree over ways to say goodbye?
When you can't really decide if you should drive or should fly?
When does a fire not start from a solitary spark?
When will you be there to light the way in the dark?

Where is the place that can keep secrets from others?
Where can we feel safe like hugs from our mothers?
Where do we carry our secrets and deepest fears?
Where will you lay your head and let loose your tears?

Who is going to gently cup your cheeks and stop the fall?
Who can see through that tough exterior wall?
Who does nothing but constantly hurt your heart?
Who will come back and never ever depart?

What shall it take to teach you a lesson?
What can it mean when you are over stressing?
What will be your happiest day ever?
What are you going to tell them that is clever?

Why do we live out of fear, til we die inside?
Why do some people only seem to collide?
Why do you offer a hand that is gloved?
Why wasn't I good enough to be loved?

THE OCEAN'S SPECIAL GIFTS

It is time to get yourself ready
Get in shape, strong and fit
What lies in front of every man
Is a voyage which needs grit.

Clean the deck with great care
For it has to be understood
That each and every crew member
Will have to have a steady foot.

If your life's rivers and oceans
Take you on voyages galore
Lock in all of the sights friend
Your soul will start to want more.

Your sails are full of gusto
Many travels still lay ahead
Dawn til dusk you keep moving
Until exhausted you lay your head.

The voyage never gets easy
In fact it becomes even harder
As you grow with each storm
You will end up going farther.

As you learn about the winds,
The dark currents that carry you
A skilled sailor you will become
Faster than on waters light blue.

Those who sail beside you
Trust their life in hands so steady
Through storms and white waters
To arrive home safe at the jetty.

To push you past your limits
And to make decisions swift
So you can endure anything
Are the ocean's precious gifts.

THE RESCUER

Life can be so awfully cruel
Stacking it all up against you.
As you grow up lacking love
Your feelings are not at all true

The times you spent alone and sad
Were not always the best
Relationships are like lesson plans
At the end there's always a test.

Learn your lessons or repeat them
So does the old saying goes
No matter how much you love someone
If they don't want to dip their toes.

In times of chaos you stand tall
And let them know you care
Your umbrella is full of holes
The rain will soak your hair.

You cry in secret and curl up so
The pain turns you into dirt
Frowns turns to laughter as you stand
Kids run and hide in your pleated skirt.

As you carry on with your life's work
Many more you will surely save
Just remember the time it took
To rescue you from same.

You have helped the countless masses
With deed, thought and skill
Who will rescue your lonely soul?
In the end perhaps someone will!

THEY ARE NOT COMING

You sit and drink your glass of water
Wondering where they are
Meeting time has come and gone
They couldn't be that far.

You both agreed to take a chance
To see if your puzzles actually fit
You think to yourself "Is it me?"
It wasn't you who seemingly quit.

You are the one who keeps their word
When you say it, you are honor-bound
Your "friend" has no couth and your
Cell phone does not make a sound.

Are they ok? Should I call them?
Questions race through your mind
But you know deep down inside
They are not coming tonight.

TRY

It's not easy to open up again
After countless trials and fails
The only way a sailboat moves
If the crew unfurls all its sails.

So get moving and figure it out
How you are going to open up
The secret is to learn to drink
Tea from an empty cup.

The best way to connect again
Is to share what makes you you
It's not about the money you have
More like "Is your heart still true?"

It's not about the things you have
Or the heights to which you soared
But rather about how you stood
With the weak, the needy, the ignored.

As you take a deep breath again
Your words are your best tools
Attempt to block out distractions
And ignore advice from fools.

Listen to what they are really saying
Not the fluff that's all around
Stare into the heavens and dream
But anchor your feet on solid ground.

Never ever stop to boast or gloat
And to stop and push out your chest
Moments like that make you vulnerable
Keep on grinding! That's the best.

In terms of how it all feels
When you cross the finish line
A new race waits around the corner
The one thing you can't buy is time.

WALK WITH ME

She wakes up each morning with stars in her eyes
Makes me want to kiss her, I don't think she tries.
I see the stars' reflections as we slowly kiss
The thought of not touching her is opposite to bliss.

We hold hands in the cold, the heat and the dark
As our steps start to synchronize on those walks in the park.
Some people grow closer through years of outings and dates,
Our story is shorter; we know we have one fate.

The lingering feelings of our hearts' echoed bruises
Remind us how not to be and what is so useless.
So we don't make promises that neither can't keep
And relish all the other moments that aren't deep sleep.

On days that the sun shines we stroll hand in hand
Avoiding potholes that lurk much like snakes in the sand.
Timing is everything, as the old adage goes
Is it too soon to ask her, who really knows?

Will you walk with me for a short little while
As the days morph into months, then years in a pile?
I have only to offer this gift which is but mine
The love of my life throughout a lifetime.

WHEN YOU DANCE WITH ME

I take your hand and pull you close
My other one finds your lower back
The steps come back as if we were one
We glide just like we were on a track.

The music reaches both of us
With each step we reinforce the beat
Locked as one we spin and move
Each movement increasing the heat.

Some people venture on the dance floor
With trepidation and fear
It's obvious to any onlooker that
We seem to belong here my dear.

Forgetting troubles, our eyes are fixed
On each other's beating heart
We sway and laugh to the music
Not wanting to come apart.

Time is on pause, as is the world
Nothing else matters but trust
Whenever we step on the dance floor
Full concentration is a must.

Hearts in synchronized tempo
The timing of each step is key
It shows how close we really are
My darling when you dance with me.

WHIRLWIND OF SMILES

You say hello as you see her walking,
She glances at you because you are gawking.
Replies softly with a wave of her hand,
Instead of moving now you just stand.

The next time you stop to exchange three words,
A warm wave of bliss slowly unfurls.
While walking away you turn to watch her leave,
She hides her nervous hand in her sleeve.

Third time there are even more words,
You both pause to listen though your head hurts.
Why would you stop at each other's look or style,
If you weren't attracted your grins would surely fly.

She alters her route to walk past you for sure,
Her motives are simple; your smile is so pure.
The last time you paused, but now you will stand still,
Talk together, laugh and grin for longer you will.

Now comes the time for the ask and the answer,
You ask her to coffee and she says yes much faster...
...Than you thought and with skillful smiles and a touch,
She confirms your idea that she likes you very much.

Laughs lead to touches and touches to a kiss,
You wonder how lovely this is; a feeling like this.
She asks you the reason why you first said hello,
"You were a whirlwind of smiles" you reply real slow.

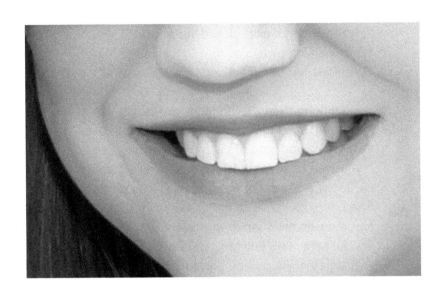

WINE WILL TELL

The selection is wide and so is the glass
You can either get Merlot or a Shiraz
How are you feeling will often tell
What your selection will be? Zinfandel?

The bouquet rises to meet your nose
Smiles are unleashed by memories of prose
You salivate slightly at what is to come
A beautiful sensory experience has begun.

You share it with friends, at time lovers
It releases your true self as you discover
The sentiments hidden, only skin deep
Always ends with a deep peaceful sleep.

The wine grows legs and not just on your glass
Verbiage oozes forth, wit and some sass
From table to living room then kitchen
Where all good parties really begin.

It's time for another bottle, or six
Let's see who resists the truthful mix
Time for dancing for fun and to show love
No need to push, bang or even shove.

Friendships turn stronger from one more glass?
Your loved one needs a kick in the ass?
Does your friend need a hand after they fell?
You can be certain that truth wine will tell.

WORK

They say patience builds your character
If you don't get what you want
Right away or as soon as you desire
It can't appear from a magic wand.

To decipher the reason behind
Why your wish was not granted
Is not as important as why you were
Left alone on the island...stranded.

You gain a minutia of experience
As you have to go, but you want to stay
Each movement of the two stones
Polishes them both in a strange way.

With the least amount of fanfare
Gather knowledge, wit and move
In the direction which you must
Get out of your usual groove.

Calculated, precise chess moves
Have the power to set you free
To move the unmovable mountain
And to slowly live... not just to be.

No matter how fast you advance
At what speed you get ahead
What matters is that you are patient
With each moment til you're dead.

Your ever-growing power
Lies in movements light as air
With strength of a thousand hammers
Land blows without hesitation or care.

Decisive actions are required
To achieve all of your dreams
The folly of most men is complacency
Ensure your kettle always steams.

YOU CAME BACK

Last time that you were in my life
It seemed more like a blur
It was a brief encounter
Between a hurt boy and a fragile girl.

Neither one of us was ready
To be part of a couple...a paired bond
We parted as friends and here we are
Holding hands, dancing, singing songs.

You reappeared in my life as if by chance
Seasoned, with lots you know
The rhythm of our fluid conversations
Seems to melodically ebb and flow.

Familiar way you hold my arm
Betrays strong feelings and then
The way our eyes dance and dart
Around and find their target again.

It seems as if we never parted
Like we were never ever away
The way your hair smelled as I held you...
I missed it, and you every day.

Here we are much older...
With no malice, nor time to spare
We stripped away the superfluous
We need honesty and deep care.

Happiness means you are by my side
No matter what's down the track
Life is short... We love one another
What matters is that you came back.

YOU LEAN IN

When you have the chance to prove to them
That you are steady and strong,
Don't let the shades of fear gain power
And push you down the hole.

The times when you can prove your worth
To the one you love the most,
Step up to the plate with courage,
Make contact with the ball then smile as...
...you lean in.

When you have the choice to lean right out
And pull away from all that's love,
Will you stand right next to him and
Show that he is irreplaceable?

He lacks the forethought to figure you out
But that is not really his role,
The reason for his life is to love you
Without questioning your inner light as...
...you lean in.

He thinks of you when he goes to work
In the morning to toil at a job he hates,
You prepare his lunch that you do so well
He smiles as he takes the first bite.

A stranger hints at flirting with you
Until you furrow your brow and turn away,
You call your love and tell him how much
The thought of him excites you as...
...you lean in.

Things get hard as they do periodically
And you have a choice to make,
To allow him to feel the pain
Or to minimize it with your gentle caresses

Your bond strengthens itself...
A self-correcting loop of respect and care,
Excluding everyone else as the two of you
Glance at each other daily....and
...you lean in!

CPSIA information can be obtained
at www.ICGtesting.com
Printed in the USA
LVHW082358090419
613600LV00008B/86/P